GRANT PUBLIC LIBRARY
51 FRONT STREET
P.O. BOX 695
GRANT, MICHIGAN 49327

FROST-BITE & FROST-BARK
Robert Frost at Michigan

Robert M. Warner

FROST-BITE & FROST-BARK

Robert Frost at Michigan

Robert M. Warner

BENTLEY HISTORICAL LIBRARY
THE UNIVERSITY OF MICHIGAN

Published with the assistance of the Jay J. Seaver Fund
An endowment of the Bentley Historical Library, University of Michigan

Bentley Historical Library
Bulletin No. 47, October 1999

©1999–Bentley Historical Library
The University of Michigan
Ann Arbor

Bentley Historical Library
University of Michigan
1150 Beal Ave.
Ann Arbor, MI 48109-2113
　　phone: 734.764.3482
　　reference e-mail: bentley.ref@umich.edu
　　website: http://www.umich.edu/~bhl

Printed by University of Michigan Printing Services

Designed by Seiko J. Semones

On the cover: Photograph of Frost from *Whimsies*, Nov. 1921.
In background, Frost's acceptance of the Fellowship in Creative Arts, July 7, 1921.

Foreword

The association of Robert Frost with the University of Michigan is more than a story of a great poet in residence at a great university. That this poet should come to spend considerable time at this university signaled a realization on the part of UM and hopefully all great universities that institutions of higher learning had an obligation to foster the creative dimensions of human activity. The experience of the UM in having Robert Frost in residence demonstrated how the presence of a creative mind within the community could enrich its intellectual life. Though President Burton, who championed the idea, was never able to institutionalize it as a permanent part of the university's program, the fact that Robert Frost was here is an enduring reminder of a particular intellectual vitality on the campus during the 1920s. The idea of university sponsorship of the creative arts is a powerful one. The story of the relationship of Robert Frost to the UM is an example of the possibilities of such sponsorship. We are grateful to Robert M. Warner, former director of the Bentley Historical Library, former Archivist of the United States, former dean of the School of Information, and former director of University Libraries, that he would take time to search the archives to tell the story of this remarkable collaboration between a poet and a university. We also appreciate the work of William K. Wallach, assistant director of the Bentley Library, and of Seiko Semones, a graphic designer, for their editorial and design work in the preparation of the bulletin for publication.

Francis X. Blouin, Jr.
Director

Robert Frost portrait. Oil painted from life: Leon A. Makielski, 1923. Robert Frost Collections, Special Collections Library, University of Michigan Library.

Artists, writers, poets, musicians of world renown are a common part of Ann Arbor's cultural environment today and reflect a commitment to the creative arts as an accepted part of the University of Michigan's mission–a tradition which dates back to the Nineteenth Century. Almost from the time of founding in 1880, the University Musical Society brought artists to Ann Arbor. In the same era literary societies and similar groups were formed. Greatly enhancing this tradition was the establishment of the Fellowship in Creative Arts in 1921 which brought to Ann Arbor the distinguished American poet Robert Frost.

The story of Frost's coming to Ann Arbor is generally well known.[1] But there are a number of components that have not been explored, offering fascinating views of Frost, the University, and the beginning of a famous romance. This investigation examines how the Fellowship originated, how Frost was selected, how the activity was financed and how Frost's tenure affected the University of Michigan.

Michigan did not originate the idea of creating a fellowship for the creative arts nor of making Frost its first recipient. Credit for the idea and its implementation shifts from Ann Arbor to Oxford, Ohio, where President Raymond M. Hughes of Miami University had already established a fellowship for Percy MacKaye, poet-dramatist. At a meeting of the National Association of State Universities in Washington in November of 1920, he elaborated on his idea that colleges and universities should become the patrons of the Arts. He noted that the country was prosperous and a leader in material things, but he urged that America should not simply reflect a "Golden Age of Prosperity" but also a "Golden Age...in Art." He challenged the American university to assume the leadership of this cultural movement by establishing creative arts fellowships around the country and went on to list a number of musicians, painters, sculptors, dramatists, writers and poets (including Robert Frost) who should be sponsored by American institutions of higher education. This speech was published and circulated in the academic community.[2] Perhaps the most enthusiastic response to Hughes' idea came from Michigan's new president, Marion L. Burton. Formerly president of the University of Minnesota, Burton had been named Michigan's president in December of 1919. Tall, young (45), and very personable, he possessed a persuasive charm that stood him in good stead with his new constituencies: the Regents, faculty, students and alumni. A noted speaker, he also possessed political and administrative talent and brought energy and new vision to Michigan as he took up his position in the summer of 1920. At the Washington meeting, Burton apparently discussed Hughes' proposal with him, for he received a follow-up letter in which Hughes listed thirty-one poets, dramatists, painters, musicians and sculptors as possible "candidates for a Michigan fellowship" and suggested that "a fellowship of two or three thousand dollars will go a long way towards interesting some of these people," adding that some of them might require larger amounts. He indicated that if Burton were interested in any of the persons on his list he or his associates could quietly sound them out as to the funding they might require. Hughes was sure that if one or two institutions of Michigan's stature would

Marion Leroy Burton, president of the University of Michigan (1920 - Burton Papers, "Portraits (3)," Box 23, Bentley Historical Library, University of Michigan.

establish such a fellowship, the idea "would spread, and that something really valuable for American art could be accomplished."[3]

Burton underlined four names on Hughes' list and subsequently asked him to get more information about them and their availability. Among the four was Robert Frost.[4] Hughes responded with the information that Frost "could probably be secured" whereas the situation was not promising for the other three. In strengthening the case for Frost, Hughes noted that "Robert Frost is at present supporting himself on a New Hampshire farm as a farmer, and that certainly is an undesirable occupation for a great poet."[5]

As the year ended, correspondence concerning the fellowship continued between Burton and Hughes, focusing on Robert Frost as the candidate. On December 15 at a meeting of the Deans, Burton had won unanimous approval of the idea of establishing a fellowship in the creative arts, and the following day he ran the idea by an informal meeting of the Board of Regents where its advantages were acknowledged, but the Regents added the caveat that they hoped it would be funded by a private gift. This response caused Burton to worry about using regular appropriated funds for the appointment, a concern he passed on to Hughes. Hughes offered to sound out Frost as to his interest in the position and his terms and advised Burton that the terms of the fellowship "should be one of freedom to work at his own art without any classroom obligations." He carried out this assignment through his own artist in residence Percy MacKaye, who was also a friend of Frost's.[6] Frost responded to MacKaye conveying both his practical requirements for accepting the Michigan offer and his philosophical views on the entire concept of the fellowship. Hughes forwarded Frost's response and gave Burton further advice on handling the offer. He urged Burton to locate a house for Frost and to work out all the details of the rent and expenses so the prospective candidate would not have to bother about such things. Seeing a certain impracticality in artistic people, Hughes wrote that "there are a number of rather funny things about these artists" suggesting that the University "provide them with a house...[as] they might not have the wit and the energy to get a house and the getting of it might spoil the whole thing."[7]

For his part Frost was pleased to learn of the Michigan opportunity and the possibility that it might "rescue me from the public lecture platform for a living," complaining that he had "had to interrupt one of my best spells of writing to go out talking this winter." More specifically he suggested that, in addition to housing, he would need "$2500 to $3000," a sum that had been agreed upon at a "family conference." To reinforce the point he added that "we are a family of six, you know, still all dependent on me...."[8]

More philosophically he mused that "in the old days" support for the arts was "the favor of kings and courts; in our day I was beginning to be afraid it would have to be on women's clubs." He felt that it was a far better solution for colleges and universities to take on this responsibility. "We are sure to be great in the world for power and wealth. Our government will see to that with appropriations and tariffs. But some one who has time will have to take thought that we shall be remembered five thousand years from now for more than success in war and trade. Someone will have to feel that it would be the ultimate shame if we were to pass like Carthage (great in war and trade) and leave no trace in the spirit."[9]

After the initial enthusiasm, negotiations slowed down a bit, prompting a gentle prodding letter from Percy MacKaye singing Frost's praises as "the most ideal person for any university president to secure." He further pointed out the importance of having the right candidates for these first fellowships if there were to be any hope that the idea might be extended. Burton's assistant replied that the president was still interested in Frost but that he had been ill all the month of March and was currently tied up with the University's budget negotiations with the State Legislature where he hoped to get funding for the fellowship or to secure "a gift from some individual."[10]

Burton already had a good reputation as a fund raiser and probably felt confident in this area, but finding someone to fund the fellowship clearly became one of his principal concerns. He no doubt believed that he could raise the necessary funds, but did not know his specific target or approach. In December of 1920, he met his man. It is unlikely that he reached that conclusion at his first meeting with Chase S. Osborn, one of the state's best known citizens. Osborn had run a successful newspaper in Sault Ste. Marie, Michigan, using it as a springboard for other activities, particularly politics. He served two terms as state game and fish warden, one term as state railroad commissioner, made an unsuccessful bid for Congress and in 1908 was named a Regent of the University of Michigan. He loved this job, was good at it and became a lifelong friend of the institution. He also had time to travel widely and discover rich mineral lands in Canada, providing him the foundation for a comfortable economic position for the rest of his life.

Osborn entered the Republican primary for the governorship in 1910 on a strong progressive platform encompassing increased regulation of business, improved primary laws and workmen's compensation. By means of a vigorous stump speaking tour in Michigan's first full-scale automobile campaign, he carried both the primary and general election to become governor on January 1, 1911. His two-year term was marked by unusual success, but keeping to his campaign promise he did not run for reelection even though he played a significant role in the presidential campaign of 1912.[11]

Former Michigan Governor Chase S. Osborn about the time of his gift to the University of Michigan for the Fellowship in Creative Arts, first awarded to Frost. 1921. Osborn Papers, "Formal Portraits," Box 113, Bentley Historical Library, University of Michigan.

Burton and Osborn had met for the first time in December, 1920, when Osborn came to Ann Arbor to give a talk to the Student Christian Association. The President and the Governor took an almost instant liking to each other. Writing to Osborn after their meeting, Burton added in a postscript: "I feel as though I have known you for a long time." The following month Burton was again writing Osborn to thank him for a gift of $5000 to fund a geological expedition for Prof. William H. Hobbs, a friend of Osborn's who had personally solicited these funds. Perhaps at this time Burton began to see Osborn as a possible source of the creative arts fellowship. In any case, Burton followed with a warm letter in February and three more in April though no mention is made of the fellowship. For his part Osborn invited the President to visit him at his home and also outlined some help for the University's legislative program in Lansing.[12]

Clearly the groundwork for approaching Osborn had been done well. Now for the request. Burton saw his opportunity in a meeting he proposed to have of "a relatively small but carefully selected group of eminently successful alumni" which he arranged to hold in Ann Arbor on Saturday, May 28. Of course Osborn received one of these prestigious invitations. Even though the invitation stated that there would be "no solicitation of funds," that evidently did not apply to the Frost fellowship.[13] Burton already knew his target well and made all the right moves to win his case. Osborn was assured that "out of 50,000 alumni only 40 were invited to this meet[ing]." And further feeding Osborn's substantial ego, Burton told the governor that an invitation to this affair was a "more distinctive honor than a degree." Ego was stroked further "at luncheon when he placed me on his R." as the governor wrote his secretary. This position also facilitated convenient discussion. Osborn further told his secretary: "Also asked me about $5,000 for Robt. Frost, the poet for Pres. B." Later on in the day, President and Mrs. Burton entertained Osborn and the other guests at a reception and dinner where further discussion of the Frost fellowship undoubtedly occurred. Osborn, clearly won over by Burton, concluded his description of the event by noting that "the Pres impressed me most this time of all....Glad I came."[14]

The subject was broached but not settled. Osborn did not offer to take on this responsibility but told Burton that he was "interested in the matter and would be glad to give a thousand dollars." Burton did not pursue the funding question further because he had assured those attending "that there would be no begging and that nobody would be put in an embarrassing situation...." But in his follow-up letter to Osborn, he further explained his vision for the fellowship, noting that "it has been my thought that a real university should be a patron of art, literature and creative activity. We ought to have upon the campus persons of the rarest type of personality, men who see visions and dream dreams. Men who are actually producing the results which influence the thought of nations." Burton wrote further that these persons should not be burdened with "the mechanism of the highly complicated and organized university," such as teaching and examinations, but be free of the fetters of academe. Robert Frost, he felt, was just the right person and he knew he could be attracted to Michigan for the proposed $5,000. Burton's letter was masterful. He saw he could not pursue the additional funding from Osborn since by his $5,000 for the Hobbs expedition "you have done your share," but expressed the hope that Osborn might know someone he would be willing to approach who could make the contribution.[15]

Osborn's response could not have been more gratifying to Burton. "I am acutely interested in your desire to have Ann Arbor advanced in an artistic, atmospheric and ethical manner," Osborn wrote. "Your plan for bringing about results is a perfect one. I do not think you could start better than with Robert Frost. I admire him as in the first class of those who live in the zone of purest poetry." Then despite the fact that he could not "afford to subscribe $5000 now," backed up by a detailed explanation of his current difficult financial position, Osborn concluded: "I am going to subscribe this Frost money all myself." Explaining further: "I want the satisfaction of it and the happiness of it, and I want to give you the encouragement of my practical sympathy and support...and I wish to do it under circumstances that are not easy, because I shall appreciate it within myself all the more." All that remained were the details–could he make payment in installments and not until after October?[16]

As soon as he received the Osborn letter, Burton telegraphed his response: "Profoundly touched by your letter of June 21[.] May I announce plan during commencement week[?]Will present letter to Regents Tuesday[.]" The rest of the message assured Osborn that no funds would be needed before October and that the gift could be made in ten installments. Osborn immediately responded that the gift could be announced at any time Burton wished.[17]

The President presented Osborn's letter to the Regents at their meeting of June 28. Not surprisingly, they enthusiastically accepted the gift. Knowing the value of sharing the exquisite details with the Governor, Burton wrote him promptly: "The Board of Regents was greatly delighted with your proposition. In fact, something happened in the Board which I have not witnessed before. They have been so much interested in this plan and were so completely surprised with the contents of your letter in view of what you had already done for Professor Hobbs' expedition that the motion to accept the gift with thanks was voted by a rising vote of the members of the Board." Burton continued with a judgment that turned out to be quite accurate: "It [Osborn's gift] represents an ideal so large and so pregnant with meaning for the life of the Institution that I believe few things that you have done will bring you greater satisfaction than this one." He told Osborn that he had informed Frost of the gift and "have assurances that he will accept the call."[18]

Regent Junius Beal wrote Osborn of his colleagues' appreciation of his "generous response to the vision of fostering Art at the University by enabling us to get the poet Frost." And Osborn saw to it that the news got around. He sent a *Detroit News* article on the subject to his political writer friend, Charles White of the *New York Tribune*, who assured Osborn that it was "a right beautiful idea to have Mr. Frost 'pottering around' in the Wolverine state. It will be of great benefit to him. I'll bet he'll 'expand' some if he runs up against a certain governor up around Sault Ste.

Marie." Osborn felt so good about his gift that, after receiving a copy of Frost's acceptance letter, he paid the full amount of the Fellowship, all $5,000, in October.[19]

Assurance of the funding of the fellowship was all that Burton needed to make Frost an offer–more generous than the poet expected. Although President Hughes of Miami, the matchmaker in these negotiations, had indicated that Frost would come to Ann Arbor for $3,500, Burton was prepared to offer the entire $5,000. He telegraphed Frost the day after the Regents' meeting, officially offering him a "fellowship at the University of Michigan for the academic year 1921-22 on the basis somewhat better than you have indicated to President Hughes." The telegram was followed by a letter with further details about the Osborn gift and, in view of the fact that the proposed $3,500 was not deemed adequate to cover Frost's expenses, the promise to "treat you much better" and provide the sum of $5,000. Burton noted that he had asked Dean of Students Joseph A. Bursley to "take active steps to help secure a proper home for you next year." He urged Frost to take a trip at the University's expense to look over the situation and explore housing with Dean Bursley.[20]

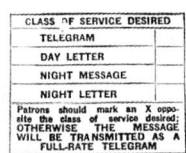

June 29, 1921.

Mr. Robert Frost
South Shaftesbury, Vermont

After correspondence with President Hughes. I desire hereby officially to offer you fellowship at University of Michigan for academic year 1921-22 on basis somewhat better than you have indicated to President Hughes. Letter follows.

M. L. Burton

President Burton conveys University of Michigan offer for Frost's initial appointment at the university, June 29, 1921. Burton Papers, Folder "6-10," Box 6, Bentley Historical Library, University of Michigan.

Frost promptly accepted by telegram. The timing of his acceptance was perfect. Commencement festivities gave President Burton the opportunity to announce to the annual meeting of the alumni on June 29 that Robert Frost would come to the University of Michigan in the fall and to stress the importance of his presence on campus. The announcement attracted the attention of the student newspaper which headlined Michigan's sponsorship of Frost as "a plan which is entirely unique in the history of state universities...." The article described Frost and the nature of his work and quoted President Burton that the student body would "benefit immeasurably from...contact with a great personality such as Robert Frost."[21]

Burton also notified President Hughes of Miami University with a telegram and a follow-up letter asking his advice on how best to use Frost. Hughes responded by urging that he have no set requirements for Frost such as teaching a class or giving a series of lectures. Let Frost volunteer for what he wanted to do, Hughes advised, and also suggested that if everything worked out with Frost Burton might raise the possibility of making his stay "a permanent matter." Hughes on the same day also wrote Frost offering best wishes on his appointment. "I feel certain," Hughes wrote Frost, "that Michigan will be a place where you will find it pleasant to be, and if this works out with Michigan for a year, I most earnestly hope that we can establish a couple more of these fellowships at other universities another year and get the proposition really on its feet as a national policy."[22]

On July 7, 1921, Frost reinforced his earlier telegram of acceptance with a gracious handwritten letter to President Burton expressing his own philosophical perspective of the Fellowship's impact:

The Frost House. Printed from a slide provided courtesy of Henry Ford Museum & Greenfield Village, Dearborn, Michigan.

South Shaftsbury, Vt.
July 7, 1921

My dear President Burton:

  You have my telegram accepting your offer. It remains for me to thank you for having chosen me to be a representative of creative literature in this way at Michigan University. We'll waive the question of whether you might not better have chosen someone else for the honor. I should have thanked you almost as much if you had. The important thing is that you should have chosen anyone. I don't know why I am so gratified unless it is because I am somewhat surprised when men of your executive authority (yours and Mr. Osborn's) see it as a part of their duty to the State to encourage the arts; and I don't know why I am surprised unless it is because I base my expectation on what I have observed of our Presidents at Washington. We have had ten or a dozen in the White House in the last fifty years, all good men and all good executives, but only one of the lot of such sight or insight. And we don't think that a large enough proportion for safety, do we?

  I can see that the appointment may contemplate the benefit of education a little as well as of poetry and one poet. You would like it to say something to the world for keeping the creative and erudite together in education where they belong. And you would like it to make its demand on the young student. He must be about some achievement in the arts or sciences while yet he is at his most creative period and the college interposes to keep the world off his shoulders. The greatest nonsense of our time has been the solution of the school problem by forsaking knowledge for thought. From learning to thinking - it sounds like a progress. But it is illusory. Thought is good but knowledge is at least no worse and thought is no substitute for knowledge. Knowledge is certainly more material to the imagination than thought. The point is that neither knowledge or thought is an end and neither is nearer an end than the other. The end they both serve, perhaps equally, is deeds in such accepted and nameable forms as the sonnet, the story, the vase, the portrait, the landscape, the hat, the scythe, the gun, the food, the bread, the house, the home, the factory, the election, the government. We must always be about definite deeds to be growing.

  This is a long letter, but you will forgive it to my wish to show my appreciation of what you and Mr. Osborn have done.

Sincerely yours,
Robert Frost[23]

Burton did not answer Frost at once since he had left for vacation in Minnesota by the time the letter arrived in Ann Arbor. But his assistant replied warmly and forwarded a copy of the Frost letter to Burton. Soon after receiving it Burton wrote Frost: "You have sensed and expressed so much more adequately than I can just the purposes which we have in mind, that it increases my anticipation of your residence among us next year." He told Frost that he had had copies of the acceptance letter sent to each member of the Board of Regents and to Governor Osborn.[24]

The announcement of Frost's coming to Michigan received some press attention focusing on both Frost and the concept of the Fellowship. Michigan's student newspaper summarized comments from faculty members at Northwestern and the University of Chicago which ranged from "we are watching the experiment very eagerly" and "it will be a great thing for Michigan" to "it would do the institution more good if the poet will give instruction in the form of regular class work."[25]

For the nitty-gritty matters pertaining to Frost's coming, Dean Bursley took his mandate from President Burton seriously and moved expeditiously to find suitable housing for the Frost family. On July 9, he wrote Frost that, although housing was hard to obtain, he had been able to rent the home of Mrs. D'Ooge, widow of Professor Martin L. D'Ooge. After consulting with Frost's Ann Arbor friend Morris Tilley, Bursley had decided that the D'Ooge home seemed to be the only place that would meet Frost's needs; furthermore it was located at 1523 Washtenaw Avenue, one of Ann Arbor's nicest streets. The rent was $150.00 monthly for a period of 9 months. "This house," wrote Bursley, "has five bedrooms and two bathrooms on the second floor and one bedroom with running water on the third floor; and there is a large attractive yard. The house is furnished but it will be necessary for you to bring your own bed and table linen, your silverware and china, (except kitchen dishes) as Mrs. D'Ooge does not rent these with her house." He also told Frost to bring some rugs along to replace those Mrs. D'Ooge was taking with her to Washington. Bursley said also that he had taken the liberty of ordering a winter's supply of coal. "We are paying a little over $15.00 a ton for coal here now, but I managed to obtain this order for you from the University at a price of $13.50 per ton." He also arranged to "have the house rent and coal paid direct by the University so that you would not be bothered by either...." Clearly the University had taken President Hughes' advice to take care of basic household problems so the visitors would scarcely have to lift a finger. There is a wonderful note in the Burton papers–a 4" by 5" scrap of paper with a penciled message from some unknown University secretary addressed to the University's second most powerful administrator, Shirley W. Smith:

> "Mr. Smith Dean Bursley says it is quite agreeable to Mr. Frost to be paid $350 a month - 9 mos.
>
> 9x350= 3150
> Rent   1350
>   4500
>
> This leaves $500 for coal and bal can be adjusted in last payment."

Scribbled in the corner of this scrap of paper was, "OK SWS 10/26". In those less bureaucratic days that seems to have been the paper work for the Frost appointment.[26]

Frost was pleased to have the appointment but he also viewed it with a touch of cynicism and a few reservations, particularly concerning his housing. He wrote his friend Louis Untermeyer that he "had been bought and paid for by an ex-governor of the state of Michigan named Osborn. Tell me it isn't true." But he assured Untermeyer that he was leaving the east "for only eight months," so there should be no break in their friendship or contact. "You can come out there [to Michigan] if you will condescend," he wrote, and, if not, Frost would come east. "I may get neighborly with Henry Ford and get a chance to bring a new car for sale over the road from Detroit to New York now and then."[27]

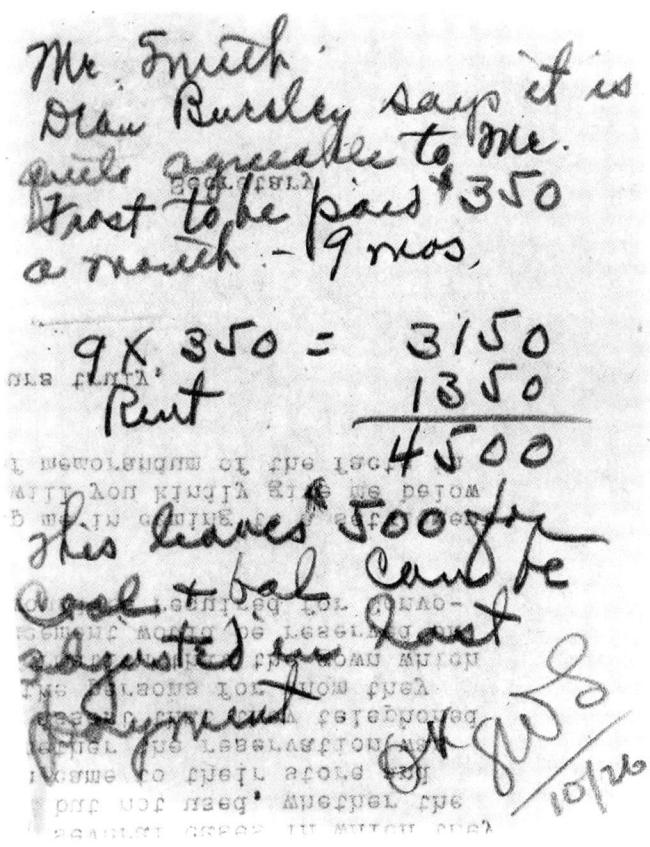

Robert Frost contract for his first year at University of Michigan. Handwritten approval by Shirley W. Smith, longtime U-M official, of Frost's contract on the back of another document. Burton Papers, Folder "6-10," Box 6, Bentley Historical Library, University of Michigan.

Frost's housing concerns centered mostly on costs. He complained to his friend Percy MacKaye: "They have rented me a house...but they ask me to buy dishes and carpets, or bring these with me....The house is very large, there'll be no hope of running it without one servant." But nonetheless he was looking forward to the year. "We've made up our minds to be in their hands for a good time....It will be a year-long picnic....There'll be music and dancing and college yelling. We all like such things. A year of them will do our digestion good and a year out of our selfish pursuits will never be missed in the long run."[28]

Despite the fact that Frost had a cold when he arrived in Ann Arbor in October, he soon was involved in a wide variety of campus activities. Helping him get acquainted was his friend, Morris P. Tilley, a professor in the English Department. He introduced Frost to his colleagues including Professor Roy Cowden who took a leading role in getting Frost involved with students. Cowden was the faculty advisor of the student literary magazine, *Whimsies*, and opened his home for staff meetings of the publication.[29] Two members of this group of students, Yuki Osawa and Stella Brunt, were among Frost's first student visitors. The women, who were close friends, became enthusiastic fans of Robert Frost. During the previous summer Stella had written her mother that Yuki had told her that Frost was coming to Ann Arbor. "I didn't believe it. It was too good to be true!" She wrote to Yuki for further confirmation but none came. Not until the opening convocation when President Burton announced that, thanks to Governor Chase S. Osborn, Robert Frost was indeed coming to Ann Arbor, did she learn that an impossible dream had come true. When Frost arrived on campus, Stella and Yuki worked up enough courage to call on their literary hero–a visit a starry-eyed Stella described in detail to her mother:

> We had neither of us ever met a writer before. We were excited underneath, like two children.
> He came to the door himself, a not-at-all-trim man of medium stature, in a not-too-well-pressed grey suit, with fair, not-too-tidy hair. He wore a shirt with a soft collar–like a railwayman at home on his Sunday off. But his blue eyes were likeable. And he was very kind and unassuming.
> He talked with us an hour and a half!
> We, Yuki and I do not believe that he will ever be a great poet. But he is a fine man. He believes in the things we believe in–not money, but the writing of what one sees in life. His first book was not published until he was thirty-eight years old! [Frost was 47 years old at this time.]
> Just to talk with him is to find new confidence....To meet and talk with a man like Frost is to be absolutely happy.
> He told us he would have us come to tea some night to meet his wife and daughter.

For their part, the young women no doubt told Frost about their *Whimsies* group and the reception they were giving him on October 21. The *Michigan Daily* reported that *Whimsies* had invited about seventy students to an informal reception where the guests would be introduced to Frost in small groups so they could have a personal encounter with the famous poet.[30]

Frost was officially introduced to the students and faculty at a reception on November 16 in the Michigan Union. The previous day, the student newspaper had given prominent notice of the reception with a photograph of Frost and a major front page article on the impending event. Consequently there was a large turnout for this Wednesday evening reception. Professor W. R. Humphries introduced Frost, who then spoke informally "about his poetry, his artistic ideas and his aims" and treated his audience to a reading of his poetry.[31]

The next evening the *Whimsies* students held their first "literary evening" in the home of their faculty sponsor Professor Roy Cowden. About twenty-five students, all aspiring writers, showed up for the event. Robert Frost "played at being 'the lion' for us," Stella Brunt wrote her mother. "We had a splendid evening, and shall have them hereafter every three weeks–but with a slightly different crowd each time. Robert Frost talked to me about fifteen minutes all alone, in a corner. It is genuine joy to be with him: one feels at once hopeless and determined. I'm going to see him at his house some day next week. I'm going to send some of my work to him...first so he can see what I try to do. Somehow I feel as though he may help me decide how I am to proceed." Stella reported another *Whimsies* evening on December 1: "...it was twelve-fifteen before I crawled in." But with more Frost meetings some of the pleasure turned into pain as the poet did a critique of her work. In January, Stella wrote her mother of a *Whimsies* evening where she "read four of my verses. It was a harrowing experience, especially when Robert Frost kept scolding at me over the same old faults–not making my meaning clear, and using old phrases. My nerves were all on edge to begin with, and that about unsettled me. I didn't sleep all night."[32]

Another member of *Whimsies* wrote a description of these evenings in the spring of 1922. Before the evening got under way they would arrange for a big wicker chair to be placed under a reading light for the guest of honor, but Frost would pass it up in favor of some "unpretentious, dim corner." As for his looks, he "appears to be quite a middling citizen–his build the least bit taller and stockier than the average, costume unostentatious (it has been a tweed suit this past season), grayish hair kept too short to swagger very temperamentally, and eyes nondescript except for their eminent kindliness. Only his forehead, broad and majestic, marks him for an 'intellectual.'" (And that term, the writer observed, Frost would "despise"). She further described the evening:

> Although he speaks lightly enough, with a whimsical, skipping surface over his comments, there is a lasting tang of significance in the stuff of them.... The conversation of Frost sparkles, more lightly, more elusively, and is at its best in the pauses–when it is in his eyes, between words. His talk proceeds so deliberately and informally that you might wonder, were you not too

absorbed for wonderment, where it was leading anyway....He is humorous and ruthless. Occasionally he mentions professorial days at Amherst....He is guilty of trifling statements that you suspect of hyperbole or irony, but his actual sturdy intent is seldom obscured....He is so very comfortable that he induces all the Whimsies in their private talk of him familiarly to call him plain "Robert" or "Frost." If I described the affection that in our hearts we think into that "Robert" he would accuse me, unjustly, of verging into sentimentality....He scorns an atmosphere of stiltedness....He has had his tussles to enliven us at times when a stifling formal silence has descended subsequent to the reading of an indifferent manuscript; but he bragged...that on need he "could make" us talk! His blunt candor, turned genial by the twinkle in his fatherly eyes, is enviable. Once in the process of criticizing a "nice obscure poem" (he is a master in subtly discriminating between his "nices," this one being strongly derogatory because coupled with the "obscure") he said meditatively, "You know–there is a difference between fetching and far-fetching...." He will often help tide over an emptiness thus....

Stella Brunt Osborn at ca. the time of her graduation from the University of Michigan, 1922. Stella B. Osborn Papers, "Early Photos," Box 34, Bentley Historical Library, University of Michigan.

Much to the delight of the group, Frost was "an excellent gossip" and shared his stories of his friends and acquaintances in the American literary establishment. One minor issue of these evening soirees was whether or not to serve refreshments. Frost opposed having them but the students and the hostess, Mrs. Cowden, went ahead with them anyhow and the student reporter noted with glee that Frost enthusiastically partook of both the punch and cookies.[33]

Clearly these regular meetings with students were a major activity during Frost's fellowship year, undoubtedly trying his patience and tiring him at times. But for those students who were fortunate to be in the group, they were unforgettable and inspirational. The first issue of *Whimsies* published after Frost arrived carried a photograph of Frost as its frontispiece with the words: "Robert Frost To Whom These Pages are Respectfully and Affectionately Dedicated." The magazine occasionally carried a Frost poem. Looking back on Frost's first Michigan year, *Whimsies* summed up his role unambiguously: "To *Whimsies*, the presence of Robert Frost at Michigan was the most significant phase of last year's University life....His influence has been mild but pervasive, kindly but corrective. We believe that not alone the literary aspect, but the entire atmosphere of the University has been improved since this great man came among us."[34]

The *Whimsies*-Frost interaction brought to the campus a series of poetry evenings by well-known poets of high standing in the literary world. The Ann Arbor branch of the American Association of University Women joined *Whimsies* in sponsoring the series which proved to be very successful. Frost's special role was to use his personal friendship with the poets if they needed additional encouragement to accept an invitation. Amy Lowell was one to receive his distinctive treatment. In addition to Lowell, the other poets who came were Padraic Colum, Carl Sandburg, Louis Untermeyer and Vachel Lindsay.[35]

Initiating the series was the Irish poet Padraic Colum who drew a good crowd in part because of the interest in the newly independent Irish Republic. After the poetry reading and commentary, *Whimsies* staff hosted a reception in Frost's home where they had a chance to meet the visitor and talk with him informally. The next poetry reading was described by Frost as "a dose of Carl Sandburg" and was most certainly not followed by a reception in his home. The two poets were not friends, as is evidenced by Frost's description of Sandburg's visit to Michigan: "He's another person I find it hard to do justice to. He was possibly hours in town and he spent one of those washing his white hair and toughening his expression for his public performance. His mandolin [guitar] pleased some people, his poetry a very few and his infantile talk none. His affectations have almost buried him out of sight. He is probably the most artificial and studied ruffian the world has had."[36]

But next in the series came Frost's close friend, Louis Untermeyer, and the mood changed. The two friends spent a good portion of time scratching each other's back. In his presentation at Hill Auditorium, Untermeyer read a number of Frost's

Vol. II, No. 3　　　　　　APRIL, 1922

WHIMSIES
MICHIGAN'S LITERARY MAGAZINE

"We make ourselves a place apart
　Behind light words that tease and flout,
—But oh, the agitated heart
　Till someone find us really out."
　　　　　　　　—Robert Frost.

poems in addition to his own and praised him as "the greatest of American contemporary poets." Frost reciprocated with equally high praise for Untermeyer at a reception for him and his wife Jean.[37]

Amy Lowell followed Untermeyer. Lowell and Frost together entertained an overflow crowd in Hill Auditorium on May 4. Frost was anxious for her to come to Ann Arbor, for he knew she would put on a good show—and he was not disappointed. "On stage she was stout, pompous, officious...sweeping her pince-nez off her capacious bosom...plucking a large pocket-handkerchief out of a hiding place in the rear of her skirt, and...bumbling about with the special reader's lamp she always carried with her." And here was where Frost became part of the show. In addition to introducing Lowell, he seemed to be in charge of her lamp. Those members of the audience close to the stage were amused by Lowell's audible whispers to Frost concerning placement of the lamp. In trying to assist her, Frost caused the lamp to blow a fuse, plunging the hall into darkness. No matter. Frost and Lowell held the audience "in howls of laughter by their impromptu jests" until the power was restored. Adding further to the levity of the evening Frost, after finishing his introduction and bowing to Miss Lowell, tripped over the reading lamp cord causing the speaker's pitcher of ice-water to upset. The audience enjoyed the show even though many were put off by her arrogance and talking down to her listeners about her work.[38]

The series ended with a bang (or perhaps a boomlay, boom) with Vachel Lindsay, another Frost friend. A real showman, he "acted out and chanted" his poems on stage. The students responded "with uncritical enthusiasm" to his performance. Lindsay was an equally great success off-stage when he charmed *Whimsies* members by having a personal visit with each one of them and doing some pen and ink drawings for the group. Many wanted Frost to end the series, but he preferred to stay in the background. His role (in addition to adjusting reading lamps) was to introduce the speakers, entertain them, and see that they met with *Whimsies* staff and other students.[39]

Frost's presence on campus brought visits from other literary figures who, although they did not give formal presentations, sometimes met with small groups in informal discussion of their craft. Stella Brunt described one of these meetings with "one of the leading...younger poets," Witter Bynner, whom Frost introduced to *Whimsies* students. On a cold February afternoon *Whimsies* and its "gang" were invited to Frost's home for a visit of more than an hour. "There were about a dozen of us....Also present was Jessie Rittenhouse, the leading poetry critic in the country....It was quite thrilling–two poets, and a critic, and a handful of college rhymesters, a small group around a blazing fire in that fine old room."[40]

Whimsies was indeed an important interest of Frost's during his stay in Ann Arbor, but he was active in other groups as well. His activities are difficult to document, but we know that he gave talks to the Unitarian Church and to the Rotary Club and that he was invited to participate in the Azazels Club, a selective club of mostly senior members of faculty. One of its members, architecture professor Emil Lorch, wrote that "the good poet was recently the guest of a little faculty club to which I belong and thus it was my good fortune to see him at rather close range. Need I say...how fine he is, and what his coming means to those interested in art...." Lorch had the audacity to compose a poem to honor the guest and, although it was not quite the quality of Frost's work, it did not discourage him from accepting membership in this group.[41]

There were other social engagements including dinner with President and Mrs. Burton. Burton wanted to have a party which would include the Frosts and his benefactor, Chase Osborn and Mrs. Osborn, but that did not work out. Osborn countered with an invitation for Burton to bring Frost to his camp on Duck Island in the St. Mary's River, but that did not work either. Burton went ahead with a fall dinner party for the Frosts with sixteen other guests. Frost clearly was the entertainment for the evening. Following dinner Burton had the guests gather in the drawing room where "Mr. Frost read some of his poetry old and new...."[42]

At another affair, a fancy dinner party arranged by a wealthy Detroit matron, brought Frost and Edgar A. Guest together much to the surprise and chagrin of Frost. Though many in Michigan may have thought Guest in the same league as Frost, Frost certainly did not share those opinions and wrote with some derision of the meeting. There were many other social occasions during the year as well as out of town engagements including a speaking engagement at Northwestern University in Chicago in December attended by Chase Osborn who reported a large audience who were "all impressed and pleased."[43]

Summarizing Frost's influence on Michigan at the end of his first year, the *Boston Herald* noted the success of the "experiment" to bring Frost to Ann Arbor. The paper praised the selection of Frost and noted the salutary effect on the literary life of the campus his presence had inspired. Even some of the local business establishments capitalized on Frost's fame. He wrote his friend Louis Untermeyer that a local "drug store advertised on a window the confection of ice cream encased in chocolate known as Frost-bite. The book-store next door not to be out done advertised my books as Frost-Bark–Very Little Worse than His Bite." For the most part, Frost's lectures and appearances received favorable publicity, but on at least one occasion he was chastised by the local press for his comments on the decimation of the Ann Arbor squirrel population due to an unexplained illness. He called the die-off a natural and "timely" phenomenon because the population was getting too numerous. He then carried the analogy to humans, implying that overpopulation was solved by war and disease–prompting the *Washtenaw Post* to editorialize on "Robert Frost's opinion of a merciful God."[44]

As the term drew to a close, there were campus evaluations to be made of the year of "Frost-bite" and "Frost-Bark." The most heartfelt and genuine came from the students themselves. On behalf of the *Whimsies* students, twenty-two of them plus their faculty sponsor, Roy Cowden, wrote to President Burton of their appreciation of the Frost year. The letter, personally delivered by Prof. Cowden, told of the group's regular meetings with Frost. "He has given to all of us," they wrote the President, "a high regard for that which is wholesome and healthy both in art and in life....We think no one could be better fitted to stand before college students." Their letter, the students assured Burton, was a "testimonial that no single influence at Michigan this year has been...more significant or more beneficial than the presence of Robert Frost." The letter concluded with the students urging President Burton to persuade Frost to return for a second year.[45]

Similar sentiments came from the faculty. Professor L. A. Strauss wrote to Burton on behalf of the English Department who were of one mind in praising Frost and the way the Fellowship had worked out. Such a sympathetic view was not surprising coming from that department, but the Dean of Engineering, Mortimer Cooley, was inspired to write that the poet "had a great and good influence on our student body this past year." The three member faculty committee to review the Fellowship, chaired by the Dean of the College of Literature, Science and the Arts, also reported favorably to the President. Speaking for the entire university community, they concluded "from all the evidence at hand...this fellowship in Creative Art has been a very great success." And no one could have been surprised at Burton's own appraisal contained in his annual report that "the experiment proved more than successful...and [the] impetus given to literary effort as the result of Mr. Frost's presence, his active participation in University life, and his peculiarly inspiring personality have been of incalculable value. The results of his efforts...are of the sort for which...it is the real aim of every true university to strive...." Burton even had half jokingly suggested at an alumni gathering that Frost might be more popular than football coach Fielding Yost. When told of this comparison, Frost suggested that the matter be put to the test by his scheduling a reading in Hill auditorium at the same time as a home football game. The result, Frost concluded, would be that no one would be in the auditorium since even he would be at the game.[46]

Climaxing Frost's University relationship was the awarding of the honorary degree of Master of Arts to him at the June Commencement. It is clear that Frost wanted this recognition and made his wishes known directly to President Burton as early as January 1922. Burton was more than happy to accede and Frost was pleased to share the Commencement activities with Secretary of State Charles Evans Hughes and other honorees. He was a bit peeved that he had not received a doctorate like Secretary Hughes but he did like his citation: "As a Fellow in Creative Arts, Mr. Frost has been a welcome sojourner in our academic community—wise, gracious, and stimulating."[47]

While Frost's public life had gone well during his Ann Arbor year, his family life had suffered its share of problems. His daughter Lesley had enrolled in the University and joined a sorority but neither brought her happiness. Her sister Irma was unhappy with Ann Arbor too. The Frost's daughter Marjorie whom they had left behind had become so lonesome and discouraged that her letters had caused her mother to make two trips to see her. Son Carol had enjoyed Michigan's successful football season but grew restless after it ended, and after an unpleasant encounter with his father in the spring, he walked out of their Ann Arbor residence and made his way back to the Frost home in South Shaftsbury, Vermont.[48]

Also clouding the picture was Frost's unhappiness with his rented home and its owner. According to his friend Louis Untermeyer, Frost "disliked the place, the name, and the owner." They had a fire in the roof of the house in April which was serious enough to bring the fire department. This was followed by trouble with Mrs. D'Ooge in settling up his account. She claimed that everything was not in proper order and that the Frosts had not been ideal tenants. Frost wrote with both humor and anger to Untermeyer that the "Widow (pronounced Dogie as in The Chisholm Trail) accused me out of a clear sky of having stolen or otherwise nefariously made away with one of the five iron pisspots she would swear she had distributed to the five bedrooms of the house....She wouldn't claim it was an Etruscan vase. Neither was it Mycenaean or Knossian ware. Nevertheless it represented a loss of fifty cents and she proposed to make a stink about it if not in it....If I did anything with it, I probably took it out into society to make conversation and lost it. I remember trying hard to break it over Carl Sandburg's head for his new mysticism and madness prepense–but in vain. I may have dented it ten cents worth. I have asked her to let the ton of coal we left her in the cellar go toward that."[49]

Despite all the adulation and excitement of the year (or perhaps because of it), Frost was tired–"exhausted" was the word his biographer used. As he was preparing to return to Vermont, Frost wrote his friend John Bartlett summarizing the year:

> This has been a year to wonder at. I don't know what I haven't done this year. I've had no assigned work as you may have heard. I've been supposed to have nothing to do but my writing and the University has been supposed to have nothing to do with me but take credit for my writing. In practice it has turned out humorously. I've been pretty busy dining out and talking informally on all occasions from club meetings to memorial services on the athletic field on Decoration Day. I have felt nonsensical at times. But it's the first year of an experiment. We want to find out if every college couldn't keep one artist or poet and the artist or poet and college be the better for the mutual obligation. There'll be less lionizing when the thing settles down and people get used to the idea."[50]

So Frost was ready to leave but he was not so tired that he did not begin consideration of what his terms should be if he were to return for a second year.

Robert Frost's year in Ann Arbor had ramifications extending beyond the University, the community, the Frost family and even the Widow D'Ooge. Unbeknownst to him, his presence at Michigan triggered an adoption, a romance and a marriage (or a romance, an adoption, and a marriage, according to the chronology of emotions involved) between two of the key figures in the Frost saga at Michigan.

As most romances do, it all began innocently enough at the fall convocation in 1921, an unlikely occasion for the beginning of a romance, to be sure, when President Burton announced Frost's coming to Michigan and thanked former Governor Chase S. Osborn for making the Fellowship possible. In the audience that momentous day was Stella Brunt, a senior *Whimsies* student from Canada, who later wrote her mother: "I went home that night and sat up till 12:30 writing to Governor

Osborn, telling him just how much it meant to some of us to have Robert Frost here." Stella's letter was sincere and sentimental–an excellent combination to touch the governor who was both. Stella subsequently reported to her mother that "Governor Osborn wrote me a nice letter in acknowledgment of mine. And then–he sent a copy of my letter to President Burton–who himself wrote to me and thanked me for expressing our gratitude and appreciation to the governor."[51]

Encouraged by Osborn's friendly response, early in the new year Stella sent him an issue of *Whimsies* which included some of her verses. He responded with compliments on her writing. In March of 1922, Osborn wrote her three letters. In two of these letters he invited her to Duck Island, his remote camp in Michigan's Upper Peninsula, and in the March 27 letter he requested: "Please let me be your friend." By the summer, letters giving details of the proposed trip to Duck Island were arriving but the trip was suddenly canceled by Osborn due to sickness. But this was only a temporary setback to the growing friendship. It is beyond the scope of this article to trace the development of the Osborn-Brunt romance, interesting though that might be. Suffice it to say that by 1924 they were on a first-name basis, seeing each other at times, and corresponding ever more frequently. Osborn and his wife separated in 1923, but did not divorce, since neither the Governor nor Mrs. Osborn condoned it. In 1927 Stella worked briefly for Osborn and in 1931 began serving as his full-time secretary. Cementing the relationship further, on April 30, 1931 Governor Chase S. Osborn formally adopted Stella Brunt, renaming her "Stellanova"–new star. Their careers and lives were then totally joined until the Governor's death on April 11, 1949. But at Osborn's death he left not an adopted daughter but a new wife. Mrs. Osborn had died on February 4, 1948. After her death the Governor annulled the adoption of Stellanova and on April 9, 1949 they were married. Two days later, the Governor died, leaving his widow, Stellanova Brunt Osborn, who lived until 1988.[52]

Not only exhausted at the end of his Michigan year, Frost was also disappointed with the amount of writing he had been able to do; yet he had already begun to consider his possible return. For its part, the University was giving the matter serious consideration at least as early as March when President Burton had begun to receive suggestions for the next holder of the Fellowship. Upon the urging of the Deans, Burton appointed a three-man committee chaired by John Effinger, Dean of the College of Literature, Science and the Arts, to draft a statement on the Fellowship. On April 13 this group reported that the Fellowship was "a very great success," that Frost had made a "distinct impression upon our student community," and that discontinuance "would be a very grave blunder." They recommended that a permanent endowment be set up and proposed a few general terms for its administration. Their message was clear: keep the Fellowship going. The Regents came to the same conclusion and at their April meeting urged that the Fellowship in Creative Arts be continued if a donor could be found to fund it.[53]

Just as in the previous year the sticking point was funding. As early as May 4, 1922, Burton had assured Frost that he wanted him to return even though "I cannot talk officially until I have succeeded in securing the funds for the Fellowship." Burton expected that a conference of "selected alumni" he had called for later in the month would produce the needed funds, but this did not happen. Once again he sought Osborn's help–not to contribute money but to approach some of his friends for support. Osborn complied but still the funding remained elusive. As late as July 25, Burton was forced to write Frost of his lack of success. August and September passed with still no prospects. But finally on October 6, Burton jubilantly wired Frost that he had secured the necessary funding for his return to Ann Arbor and that he hoped he could come in time to attend the first faculty reception of the fall. When no reply arrived by the next day, Burton again wired Frost saying the entire Fellowship program would be jeopardized if he did not accept. The second telegram brought forth an acceptance from Frost. With less than a week to get ready, Frost's family decided not to accompany him back to Ann Arbor at this time.[54]

Burton announced to the October Regents' meeting that an anonymous citizen had contributed the $5,000 needed to continue the Fellowship, whereupon the Regents promptly renewed it and named Frost its second recipient. Although at that time the donor was able to preserve his anonymity, Burton's papers reveal that it was Horace H. Rackham, whose fortune was founded in early investments in the Ford Motor Company and who along with his wife Mary became a generous benefactor of the University. This gift in fact inspired Burton the following year to enter into serious negotiations with Rackham to establish a permanent endowment fund of $100,000 to sponsor the Fellowship in perpetuity.[55]

Before he had left Ann Arbor in June, Frost had already worked out with Burton his terms for a second year, if one were to materialize. He was to have much more freedom from both social and professional commitments than in his first year–he was to spend his time more or less as he chose. And since the offer to return had come so late, Frost had already made speaking commitments to assure financial support for the fall. On October 9, Burton announced Frost's impending return, adding that the appointment "makes the University 'a leader in the arts.'" Frost made it back in time for the fall reception on October 11 where he explained to Burton that because of all the speaking dates he had made he would have to return home almost immediately and would not be back in Ann Arbor for a few weeks. He did manage to work in an interview with a *Daily* reporter assuring him that during this year's stay in Ann Arbor, he intended "to see much more of the undergraduate body than last year." He stayed only two days as a guest of Dean Bursley before returning to New England to meet his speaking schedule in Vermont and the Boston area before leaving for a strenuous speaking tour, starting in New Orleans continuing through several cities in Texas and ending in Columbia, Missouri–altogether ten engagements in fourteen days. Since all the traveling had to be done by train, it was a difficult assignment keeping him from both his family and Ann Arbor. Not surprisingly, the trip brought on a bad case of the flu or something like it and he returned at the end of November directly to Ann Arbor where Mrs. Frost was awaiting him and could take care of him. He was so ill that he was bedridden for more than a week. Mrs. Frost was comfortably settled in their new home at 1432 Washtenaw Avenue, very close to their old one, but to Mrs. Frost's mind, much more pleasant. It was, she wrote, "a smaller house, almost directly across the street from the other. It is more cheerful and homelike, and more easily taken care of than the other."[56]

Frost was depressed by his illness and frustrated by his lack of progress in producing a new volume of poetry. And when he was able to be up, these frustrations continued. In spite of the groundwork he had laid for freedom from responsibilities there were nonetheless demands upon his time to participate in social events, attend student plays and renew ties with the *Whimsies* students. They wanted his help in arranging another lecture series and urged him to attend their evenings at the Cowdens' home as he had done the year before and which he enjoyed. He did help with the lecture series but on a much reduced scale. Louis Untermeyer, Frost's good friend, was the only poet who came; the other two speakers were novelists Dorothy Canfield Fisher and Hamlin Garland. Fisher was fine but Garland a disappointment. To compensate for him, Frost allowed *Whimsies* to schedule him for a reading but the event had to be postponed due to another two-week bout of illness. There were other Ann Arbor appearances and he agreed to be a judge for a *Whimsies* sponsored poetry contest which did not excite him. He had left Ann Arbor for both his Christmas and Spring vacations. Because of his travels and frequent illnesses–Frost claimed to have had the flu five times that winter–Frost's second year did not have the impact of the first. As he confessed: "I've been fairly absent from Ann Arbor this year and not half the sensation in the Michigan papers I was last year." Even his most ardent supporter, President Burton, admitted: "It is quite evident that last year was in some respects not as satisfactory as the first year. Mr. Frost's illness contributed to this result. His creative work (a book will appear this fall) made it impossible for him to be as available for the public as during the first year."[57]

And the University's senior regent, Junius Beal, dourly commented: "Regarding the Fellowship in Creative Arts....From the standpoint of the students the fine, natural sweet spirit of Edgar A. Guest would have helped much more than Frost to inspire and spiritualize."[58]

But Frost's *Whimsies* friends were unshaken in their view of him. Senior Lawrence Conrad, who assisted Frost with typing the manuscript of his book of poetry, wrote President Burton that the Fellowship in Creative Arts "made it possible for me to come into contact with Robert Frost, and this contact has enriched my University career beyond any other single factor. I have seen, during my junior and senior years, a new, sound and praiseworthy spirit taking possession of the University, somehow touching every person in it...." He gave Frost credit for the lecture series and for making *Whimsies* flourish. The official record was equally positive with the *President's Report* noting that in his second year, "as before his presence has proved an inspiration to the fortunate students who have experienced his kindly encouragement and have been privileged to benefit by his ripe wisdom and personal charm. In the truest sense, the informal labors of such a man are education." Frost left Michigan in early June 1923 for South Shaftsbury to work on his still unfinished book of poetry and to receive a visit from the new president of Amherst asking him to return to their faculty.[59]

Frost's leaving Ann Arbor, however, did not mean the end of the Fellowship in the Creative Arts nor the end of Michigan's interest in Robert Frost. The Fellowship was still high on President Burton's list of priorities. He wrote the Dean of the College of Literature, Science and the Arts how important he believed it was to carry on the Fellowship and to find a distinguished person to accept it. It was especially important that this third Fellow be outstanding because, he explained: "There is, I find, in some quarters a little feeling of dissatisfaction with the past year" although he added, "I am not at all in sympathy with that feeling." For candidates Burton listed among possible Americans: Sinclair Lewis, Eugene O'Neill, Edward Arlington Robinson and Stephen Vincent Benet. His even longer British list included Kipling, Shaw, Masefield, Yeats and Noyes. Burton already was inclined to favor his British list and indicated that he might extend the invitation himself. In a similar vein, following up his letter to Dean Effinger, he wrote two University Regents of his continued aim to enhance cultural values at Michigan. He noted that the state was doing a good job supporting the University and called attention to the highly successful building program it was making possible. But that was not enough to make a great University. "In a word, we want to have discriminating people everywhere understand that the University of Michigan, tax-supported, has just as much appreciation of the finer things of life as does Harvard or Yale." Then he put the continuing of the Fellowship in the Creative Arts at the top of his list of steps to foster this appreciation. He said he felt "almost positive" that the donor he had interested (Horace Rackham) would endow the fellowship with a $100,000 gift. Burton stated that his goal now was to attract "one of the most outstanding literary men of the English speaking world" as Frost's successor. To do this Burton proposed to go to England to look for this person himself.[60]

Burton did go to England and although no one on his list was selected, the next holder of the Fellowship was Great Britain's poet laureate, Robert Bridges. Bridges arrived on April 4 and was introduced to the student body at a large convocation in Hill Auditorium. Frost, who had arrived a few days earlier for a poetry reading, met him too and in 1962 he humorously reminisced that he had been asked to come in order to reassure Bridges that the "western boys" weren't to be feared. Bridges' stay turned out to be a short one. At 80 years of age he perhaps came to the University too late and gave too little. He received many invitations to numerous activities, but declined virtually all of them. After three months he left the "western boys" and returned to England.[61]

Hardly had Bridges sailed for England when Burton started recruiting for the 1924-25 academic year. And Frost was one of the first he turned to for advice. He met with Frost in New England twice in July of 1924 and reported that Frost's first choice was Willa Cather and his second, Edward Arlington Robinson. He was negative to the suggestions of Burton and his faculty advisors–Augustus Thomas, Owen Wister and Winston Churchill. "He regards them all as belonging to another period and no one of them as first class material." Burton followed Frost's suggestion and visited Robinson but both he and Robinson agreed that the poet did not quite fit the job description. "He is a very difficult man to talk with" reported Burton, adding that "Calvin Coolidge is positively garrulous when compared to Mr. Robinson." Burton personally favored pursuing the Cather suggestion but found his faculty committee "strongly opposed to [a] woman." Frost concluded that she would have to be dropped from consideration–"Wouldn't be fair to Willa Cather to call her in the face of too much opposition." Other suggestions were made including Eugene O'Neill but Burton reported that both Frost and Robinson had reservations about him. Burton asked Frost to sound out Walter Eaton but Frost believed that Eaton already had too many engagements and suggested Jesse Lynch Williams instead. Acceding to his advisory committee, in October 1924 Burton offered the position to George P. Baker, a leader in the theater at Harvard, but he declined.[62]

In all these negotiations Burton kept in close touch with Frost and urged that his colleagues working on the selection do likewise because there was a larger agenda at work–to get Frost back to Ann Arbor on a permanent basis. As Burton explained to Dr. Frank Robbins, who was assisting in the search, "I would not want anyone appointed to the Fellowship which would seem to be an offence to him [Frost], because of the larger plans which we have made with him for another year, I hope." This long term plan envisioned "a super-fellowship, that is to say with the idea that Mr. Frost will come to us permanently as Fellow in Letters."[63]

After leaving Ann Arbor Frost began to miss it especially the people he had met there. In February he wrote to his friend Morris Tilley that he had "got to be a good deal more Ann Arboreal than I should suppose I could have at my age. A few people and streets and a lot of the outlying landscape are pretty well incorporated in me." He told Tilley that he would be back in Ann Arbor at the end of March and he would want to meet with his Whimsies friends. And in a later letter to Tilley, Frost indicated the kind of proposal that would bring him back: "If someone had asked me to give one seminar a week out there as long as I wanted to stay for $5,000 a year I should have taken him up." And he added: "I liked the folks. I made more and closer friends than I ever did before."[64]

Actually, negotiations to bring Frost to the University on a permanent appointment may have been actively pursued on the trip to Ann Arbor with Mrs. Frost from March 30-April 4. Frost's biographer, Lawrance Thompson, describes such negotiations. Certainly by the summer the topic was thoroughly covered by the

Burton-Frost conversations in early July. Burton described in considerable detail his negotiations with Frost to his supporter, Dean Effinger of the Literary College, who had asked for an extra $6,000 in his budget to bring Frost to his faculty. Burton reported to him that he came from these meetings with Frost "more convinced than ever that we are very wise in planning to secure Mr. Frost as a permanent member of our staff." But he cautioned Effinger that he could not be treated as a conventional faculty appointment. "We shall have to recognize frankly that we are dealing with an unusually rare spirit and that we cannot fit him into an organization precisely as most of us go into it. This principle is fundamental in the whole discussion." This meant specifically that he did "not want and will not accept a teaching professorship." What Frost did want was "a position in which he will be known as 'Fellow in Letters' and in which he will give himself in very real ways to the students and the University but never by mechanical or scheduled methods. He is willing to have a 'Seminar' for one semester each year in which he would meet a relatively small group of selected students." These were discussed not as demands but conditions which Burton "dug out of him with great difficulty in the hope of finding what arrangement would attract him to us. Frankly he said to me that what attracted him was 'the honor of it'. Our conferences were to me among the most satisfying I ever had. He opened up his heart in a very unusual way. No one who heard it all could possibly misinterpret his spirit or ideals not even when he alluded to the honor involved." Although the two negotiators had not discussed finances, Frost was willing to come to Michigan in the fall of 1924 but "in response to an almost pathetic appeal" by President Olds of Amherst he had agreed to stay until the end of the 1924-25 academic year. Effinger received this full report from the President quite positively but like any conscientious dean cautioned that "it would be necessary to take the English Department into our confidence and gain its approval before taking the final steps."[65]

Negotiation between Frost and the University progressed smoothly. Frost wanted no public announcement of his move until he had time to tell President Olds--a task that he did not look forward to and worried over to the extent that it affected his health, according to his biographer Thompson. As Frost explained to Burton, "They have been very good to me at Amherst and I must part friends with them." At Burton's request Dean Effinger convened his Literary College Advisory Board to examine the terms of the Frost proposal which they unanimously approved. "There was a general feeling of elation at the thought that such an arrangement might be possible." And Effinger added his own personal view that the appointment "will make one of the great steps in advance in the history of this institution."[66]

By October, Burton was ready to formalize Michigan's offer of a permanent appointment for Frost. In a three-page letter, he spelled out in detail all of the terms of their many discussions. Essentially there was only one item which Frost and Burton had not settled. The University expected Frost to teach one seminar a year; Frost countered with a proposed teaching load of one seminar every other year. Burton held firm on this point but in the most diplomatic terms. "Speaking in general," Burton wrote, "I have an impression that there would be greater satisfaction both to you and to the University if this should be done one semester each year, rather than every other year." Also the annual visiting fellowship would continue with the expectation that Michigan would "appoint the man whom you think would fit best into the situation here." Burton went on to say "I have an impression that with you occupying the regular Fellowship in Letters it would be wise for us to have younger men or women ... in the annual rotating Fellowship." Thus Frost was assured of little competition. This letter was the first to spell out the financial terms. It was based on action taken by the Board of Regents at their September 24 meeting. Regent Walter Sawyer moved that Frost be extended an offer to assume "the post of Fellow in Creative Arts on a permanent basis with a stipend of $6,000 per year out of University funds" and that it begin with the year 1925-26. The motion was then passed by the Board. In his letter, Burton offered Frost an annual salary of $6,000. Burton pointed out that the minimum salary for full professors was $4,000 and the average salary for this group was about $5,000. He urged Frost to make the necessary notifications of this new appointment so that Michigan could soon issue "a rather dignified announcement from this quarter." Burton concluded his long letter with what was obviously a most sincere observation: "I think you understand how very deeply interested I have been in this whole enterprise and I want you to know with what keen anticipation I shall look forward to your coming among us." This was almost an understatement. It is no exaggeration to say that this appointment was almost entirely due to Burton. On October 10, Burton announced Frost's proposed return, scheduled for September 1925.[67]

Frost's acceptance of Michigan's offer was noted at the November meeting of the Board of Regents and his appointment at Michigan and resignation from Amherst were noted in the press. The stories were flattering, if not always accurate, as evidenced by the Boston *Evening Transcript*'s assertion that the appointment carried no teaching obligations. But public announcement of his plans put an end to the secrecy and freed Frost emotionally. Michigan for its part called Frost's selection its most significant faculty appointment.[68]

Frost told his Ann Arbor friend Prof. Louis Straus the reason the Fellowship was attractive was that he liked to educate, he liked the salary and he liked the honor. "I rather like honors. But what exerts the main attraction in Ann Arbor is simply friends." By December he was telling another Ann Arbor friend, Professor Robert M. Wenley, that he was "beginning to let go here" and focusing more on the upcoming move to Ann Arbor, concluding, "We are glad to be taken back."[69]

But before Frost's return the chief patron and father of the Frost connection at Michigan, Marion L. Burton, died on February 18, 1925. Though not a total surprise since Burton had been ill with a combination of heart problems, pneumonia and other complications, nevertheless his death was a great shock on campus and nationwide. Frost did not come for the funeral but early in April, Acting President

Alfred Lloyd, writing on behalf of the University and Mrs. Burton, asked him to be the principal speaker at a memorial convocation the University planned to hold before the students left for the summer. Frost could largely control the date but Lloyd pointed out that the Regents were in Ann Arbor for their regular meeting on May 28 and suggested that that might be a good time. Everyone felt Frost was the person for this sad assignment because everyone knew "that Dr. Burton had a real affection for you." Frost replied by telegraph that he "had never before done such a thing" and that he was not an orator. "Candidly I think someone better fitted should have the honor." But despite these protests, he agreed to speak.[70]

The memorial service took place on Thursday evening, May 28. Four thousand people filled Hill Auditorium to listen to Frost eulogize Burton. Frost was the program. After an introduction by Acting President Lloyd, Frost gave not a true eulogy but a conversational, informal talk paying tribute to Burton as a great administrator who had worked well with the Legislature and a great teacher who had fostered great teaching. He then proceeded to place "many of his own personal opinions concerning education in the mouth of the dead President Burton."[71]

Burton's death placed a huge cloud over Frost and his return to Michigan, but nonetheless he went about the business of carrying out his new assignment. He wrote his friend Tilley to enlist his help in finding a house, suggesting a location not too close to campus, perhaps off Geddes. This letter was written before Burton's death for Frost noted that he knew Burton was seriously ill. On March 17, he asked Tilley to consult with Dean Bursley on the suitability of a house at 1223 Pontiac Road, with an annual rent of $700. Frost thought the location was ideal and the low rent would enable him to afford an automobile. The rental may have been confirmed when he gave a poetry reading in Ann Arbor in April. In any case, the Frosts took the Pontiac Road house and were pleased with it. It was a handsome nineteenth century cottage that well fitted their needs and taste; it was later purchased by Henry Ford and moved to Greenfield Village. The Frosts traveled by train to Ann Arbor and were pleased to stay with their friends Dean and Mrs. Bursley until their furniture, shipped by freight from Amherst, arrived. Mrs. Frost was not in robust health nor were the Frost children, leading to anxiety on Mrs. Frost's part and reluctance to leave the East.[72]

But their Ann Arbor welcome was warm. Frost was now even more famous. His *New Hampshire*, much of it written in Michigan and in part dedicated to Michigan and Vermont, had brought him a Pulitzer Prize. And his unique appointment and solo performance at Burton's memorial service gave him much status upon his return. The Frosts were among the first guests of the new president, Clarence Cook Little, a New Englander who had come to Michigan from the presidency of the University of Maine. Unlike Burton, his background was in science, not the arts or humanities. Mrs. Little, however, wrote poetry and was especially pleased with Frost's appointment. Not quite so pleasing to Frost was her idea to form an informal group of non students to share literary adventures. He did agree to participate, however. He continued with the campus literary group and attended the first fall meeting of *The Inlander*--the successor to *Whimsies*. He remembered several students from his earlier years at Michigan–among them, Mary Cooley, Dorothy Tyler and Sue Bonner, whom he later nicknamed "the three graces"–and helped them with their own magazine, the *Outlander*. There were, of course, other student contacts as well as a fall lecture tour which took him from New England to North Carolina and also tired him out and led to a bout of sickness.

While Frost was sick in Michigan his children were sick back East. Mrs. Frost had to leave Ann Arbor to take care of daughter Marjorie who was hospitalized with pneumonia. Her health problems continued, causing Frost to go back East in the middle of December. Along with these personal problems were professional disappointments. Little was no Burton. And the new emphasis on science did not replicate the warm environment that Burton had nurtured around Frost. Some of Frost's academic experiences weren't that happy either. He told a visiting friend of a meeting with teachers the previous evening in which he said he had quarreled with all of them. By the first of the new year Frost was writing his friend John Bartlett that he was having serious reservations about his permanent Ann Arbor commitment. "I am not sure of hanging on long at Ann Arbor though the position is supposed to be for life. It's too far from the children for the stretch of our heart strings....We don't like to be scattered all over the map as long as we don't have to be. Elinor stands being separated from the children worse than I do. What I want is a farm in New England once more."[73]

Because of Marjorie's continuing health problems, Frost stayed in the East with his family. He did not make the opening of the term, wiring Dean Effinger: "Fully intended to be back with my family for opening of term but doctor refuses to let us move Marjorie yet[.] Arriving myself Tuesday anyway." He explained further to Louis Untermeyer in a gloomy letter of February 11 that he had been away from Ann Arbor for two months because of Marjorie's illness, noting that Mrs. Frost was still with her, but he felt he had to come back "to make some show of teaching a little for my year's pay....All this sickness and scatteration of the family is our fault....We ought to have gone back farming years ago or we ought to have stayed farming when we knew we were well off." But Frost again had to leave because of Marjorie's illness and Dean Effinger wrote to give him warm support and encouragement.[74]

Frost did return to Ann Arbor to fulfill his agreement with President Burton to teach a seminar the second semester–his only formal obligation. Enrollment was limited to twelve students, all of whom had been screened by the chairman of the English Department. Among the twelve were his three favorites Cooley, Bonner, and Tyler. They met first in a seminar room in the library. Frost tolerated drop-ins but after three sessions he announced that he saw no need of meeting formally anymore and proposed instead that each compose a literary work of his or her own and when it was ready to be looked at to arrange a personal meeting with Frost at his home. This automatically eliminated all the non serious students and gave Frost freedom from a rigid schedule. As to his teaching methods, Sue Bonner Wolcutt later recalled: "They were, of course, non-existent. He merely talked about poetry; sometimes he talked about the technique, sometimes about the fashions in poetry. As always with Mr. Frost, what he said today he might contradict next week....We were supposed to show him our poetry for his criticism, but he never criticized it very much one way or the other. Just among ourselves we secretly believed that he wasn't much interested in our poetry, and for some reason we didn't mind at all." Mary Cooley recalled that he never criticized her poems.[75]

At winter's end, Mrs. Frost returned to Ann Arbor with the still recovering Marjorie and her sister Irma. Their return boosted Frost's spirits and also led to a romance for daughter Irma but it did not change the direction of his thinking. Among Frost's spring visitors was Amherst President George D. Olds, carrying an attractive offer which Frost accepted and proceeded to work out the terms. Robert Frost's days at Michigan were now virtually over. In retrospect his third year at Michigan had peaked at the Burton memorial service. His impact as a permanent member of the faculty was certainly not profound, although he still remained popular with the serious literary students, or at least with the "three graces." After the fanfare of his first two years, the third term was anti-climactic. Frost summarized it himself when he wrote to John Bartlett:

> We're going east again said the pendulum. This was no go this year, or rather it was too much go and what wasn't go was come. Marjories[sic] long illness (means more than sickness) kept Elinor with her in Pittsfield Mass and me commuting for months. Every week or so I would run the water out of the pipes and leave the house here to freeze. It wasnt exactly in the contract that I should be away all the time and I wasnt quite all. I'm not going to try to keep it up here with the children back there and such things likely to happen again. And anyway I want a farm. It's all arranged so you neednt exclaim a protest about such whiffling. Amherst, Dartmouth, Bowdoin and Connecticut Wesleyan are going to give me a living next year for a couple of weeks in each of them. The rest of the time I shall be clear away from the academic, feeding pigeons hens dogs or anything you advise for the pleasure or profit in it....I like Michigan people and I like Michigan. Only only.[76]

Frost's academic experience at Michigan clearly supports John Updike's recently expressed conclusion that "Frost...had wriggled or quarreled his way out of every academic post he...had, though his appetite for instructing others was powerful." Nevertheless Robert Frost did not completely forsake Michigan. He was on the Michigan payroll at least two more times. In 1927 the University paid him $500 to lecture and to advise. Before he arrived he wrote Mary Cooley to sign up for "my

The Frost house was moved to Greenfield Village where it was restored. The structure is now known as the Ann Arbor House. Photograph courtesy of Anne Percy Knott, 1998.

one-hour-a-week for one-week-in-the-year course in creative creation." He urged Mary to recruit Sue Bonner and Dorothy Tyler to sign up too. He wrote that he had "half-a mind to ask Mrs. Little to have it at her house since she turns out to be so much one of us." The next year the University hired him again for another appearance so he spent a week in March in town and again in December. There were a scattering of other appearances and contacts through the years culminating in a special convocation in April of 1962 and an honorary degree in June of that year. As he grew older Frost remembered his Ann Arbor days with warmth and affection and he cherished the friendships he had made there among students and faculty. When Mary Cooley wrote to him in 1961 to tell him of the death of Roy Cowden, he responded: "How nice of you to remember how much I cared for Roy Cowden and his country thoughts." And added the further reminiscence: "You and Sue Grundy [Bonner] and Miss Tyler were the three graces of my seminar, I assure you.[77]

In April of 1962, an old and tottering Robert Frost made his final appearance at Hill Auditorium. The bright lights of the stage bothered him but he performed to an appreciative audience of students not unlike those Michigan students he had addressed more that fifty years ago. He read his poetry and captivated his audience by looking back affectionately, with humor and with remarkable historical accuracy, at his Ann Arbor days. He spoke with real warmth of his great friend and sponsor, President Burton. But he gave President Hughes of Miami due credit for initiating the idea of the creative arts fellowship. He talked about the D'Ooge house on Washtenaw and affectionately of the "little house on Pontiac Street....It was a very pretty little thing made altogether out of black walnut. The whole house, timbers

Robert Frost at the Pontiac Street house in Ann Arbor, ca. 1925-26. Photograph by Jean Paul Slusser. Robert Frost Collections, Special Collections Library, University of Michigan Library.

and all was black walnut. It was what is called hen and chicken architecture...a large middle with two wings...a very pretty little house...a very charming house." And he chuckled at the fact that Henry Ford had moved it to Greenfield Village. Nostalgia for the past was the dominant theme of this performance. Complementing his Hill presentation was a small luncheon arranged by the University with a scattering of surviving students and friends from the old days. Mrs. Roy Cowden was there. So were Mary Cooley and Dorothy Tyler–two of the "three graces", Mrs. Campbell Bonner, Mrs. Louise Tilley Schneider, Fred Black and Stellanova Brunt Osborn–admiring student of Robert Frost and widow of Chase S. Osborn, whose money had made it all possible. Stellanova's presence, in a way, brought this reunion to its full circle. No one knows how the conversation went but we can be assured there was a lot of reminiscing and for a little while they all got to relive a bright and exciting moment in their lives.[78]

So what was the ultimate impact of Robert Frost at Michigan? Certainly the great expectations of the experiment were not fulfilled. Other colleges and universities did not fall into line and become sponsors of creative artists to enrich the culture of America. The experiment remained largely a Michigan venture and even then President Burton's dream of a permanent, fully endowed Fellowship in Creative Arts was not realized. The endowment did not materialize and the fellowship survived only a short time after Burton's death. And Burton's dream of adding Frost to the permanent faculty never came true. Nevertheless it was a noble experiment that had a significant impact on the University. It brought much publicity to Michigan, helping to stamp it on the cultural map of the country. Already renowned for its athletic prowess, the University of Michigan became equally well known for its cultural significance.

Frost-bite and Frost-bark were felt at Michigan in the 1920's and left their mark permanently on the students and the University as a whole. The presence of Robert Frost excited the campus intellectually and for the students who had personal contact with him it was, for most of them, the greatest experience of their lives. And Robert Frost himself was broadened by the experience. He wrote important poetry here and made lasting friendships. He had become "Arboreal" in spite of himself.

But the real hero of this story is actually not Robert Frost, but Marion Leroy Burton, a great president who not only significantly enlarged and improved the physical campus of the University of Michigan but greatly enhanced the intellectual vitality of the University. The endowment that Burton was working on with Horace Rackham did not come about, but the foundation was laid for the huge gifts that the Rackhams would later make to the University. The Fellowship in Creative Arts was Burton's program. Robert Frost's presence on the campus of the University of Michigan was clearly his doing. We can only guess what might have happened with Frost, the Fellowship, and the intellectual life of the University if Burton had lived. Chances are good that all would have flourished.

Robert Frost Academic Appointments: 1917 - 1963

1917-20: Professor of English, Amherst College

1921-23: Fellow in Creative Arts, University of Michigan

1923-25: Professor of English, Amherst College

1925-26: Fellow in Letters, University of Michigan

1926-38: Professor of English, Amherst College

1939-40: Ralph Waldo Emerson Fellow in Poetry, Harvard University

1941-43: Fellow in American Civilization, Harvard University

1943-49: George Ticknor Fellow in the Humanities, Dartmouth College

1949-63: Simpson Lecturer in Literature, Amherst College

EVENING IN A SUGAR-ORCHARD

By Robert Frost

From where I lingered in a lull of March
Outside the sugar-house one night for choice,
I called the fireman in a quiet voice
And bade him leave the pan and stoke the arch;
"O fireman, give the fire another stoke
And send more sparks up chimney with the smoke."
I thought a few might tangle (as they did)
Among bare maple boughs and in the rare
Hill atmosphere not cease to glow,
And so be added to the moon up there.
The moon, though slight, was moon enough to show
On every tree a bucket with a lid
And on black ground one bearskin rug of snow.
The sparks made no attempt to be the moon;
They were content to figure in the trees
As Leo, Orion, and the Pleiades.
And that was what the boughs were full of soon.

*Sincerely yours,
Robert Frost*

Frost began this poem in March 1920 while living in Franconia, New Hampshire. In Ann Arbor for the 1921-22 academic year, he revised the poem and presented it to *Whimsies*, a student literary magazine, for its November 1921 issue. It later appeared in Frost's *New Hampshire* (1923).

Endnotes

[1] See Erath Matheson, "Robert Frost as 'Poet in Residence' at the University of Michigan," *Studies in the History of Higher Education*, Claude Eggertsen, ed. (Ann Arbor: University of Michigan School of Education, 1950), pp. 24 30; Jeffrey Meyers, *Robert Frost, A Biography* (Boston: Houghton Mifflin Co., 1996), Chapter 10; Lawrance Thompson, *Robert Frost: the Years of Triumph, 1915-1938* (New York: Holt, Rinehart and Winston 1970), Chapters 13-20.

[2] *Fellowships in Creative Art in the Colleges and Universities of America*, Pamphlet in the R.M. Hughes Papers, Miami University Archives, Oxford, Ohio. Hughes apparently got the idea from his academic neighbor, President W. W. Boyd of Western College who had brought two musicians to his campus just prior to America's entry into World War I and called this innovation to Hughes' attention. Hughes quickly saw merit in the idea and "became its ardent champion." Arthur Wickenden, *Pioneering Ventures*, "Raymond M. Hughes: Leader of Men" (Oxford, Ohio: Alumni Association, 1966), p.39.

[3] Hughes to Burton, Nov. 17, 1920, Marion L. Burton Papers, Bentley Historical Library, University of Michigan hereinafter cited as Burton Papers.

[4] The other three names Burton underlined in addition to Frost were poet George Edward Woodberry, painter Edmund C. Tarbell and sculptor Paul Manship. *Ibid*.; Burton to Hughes, Dec. 2,1920; Hughes to Burton, Dec. 6, 1920, Burton Papers.

[5] Hughes to Burton, Dec. 6, 1920, Burton Papers.

[6] University of Michigan, *The President's Report, For the Year 1920-1921* (Ann Arbor, 1922), p.54; Burton to Hughes, Dec. 21, 1920; Hughes to Burton, Dec. 28, 1920 Burton Papers.

[7] Hughes to Burton, Jan. 26, 1921, Burton Papers.

[8] Robert Frost to Percy [MacKaye], Jan. 17, 1921, enclosure with Hughes to Burton, Jan. 26, 1921, Burton Papers.

[9] *Ibid*.

[10] Percy MacKaye to Burton, March 11, 1921; Assistant to the President to MacKaye, April 5, 1921, Burton Papers; Frost was 47 years old in 1921 and had already published three books of poetry by this time: *A Boy's Will* (1915), *North of Boston* (1915), *Mountain Interval* (1916), Lawrance Thompson, *Robert Frost: The Years of Triumph, 1915-1938* (New York: Holt, Rinehart and Winston, 1970), p.717 hereinafter cited as Thompson, *Frost 1915-1938*.

[11] Robert M. Warner, *Chase Salmon Osborn, 1860-1949* (Ann Arbor: Michigan Historical Collections Bulletin No. 10, Jan. 1960), *passim*.

[12] Burton to Chase S. Osborn, Dec. 13, 1920; Jan. 10, Feb. 19, April 7, April 22, April 25, 1921; Osborn to Burton, April 28, 1921, Chase S. Osborn Papers, Bentley Historical Library, University of Michigan, hereinafter cited as Chase Osborn Papers.

[13] Burton to Osborn, May, 3, 1921; Osborn to Burton, May 6, 1921, Chase Osborn Papers.

[14] Osborn to Mary F. [Hadrich], May 28, 1921, Chase Osborn Papers. This extraordinary documentation of Burton's actual asking for the gift is contained in a hand-written letter to Osborn's long-time secretary on Michigan Union letterhead, apparently right after the luncheon concluded but before the evening reception and dinner. Osborn also asked Hadrich to send Burton a copy of his autobiography, *The Iron Hunter*.

[15] Burton to Osborn, June 14, 1921, Chase Osborn Papers.

[16] Osborn to Burton, June 21, 1921. Most of the Osborn-Burton correspondence is duplicated in both the Osborn and Burton papers but the original of this letter does not appear in the Burton papers, probably because Burton transmitted the original to the Board of Regents. Until Osborn's letter arrived, Burton was very unsure that he could carry this off. As late as June 14, he was writing his friend President Hughes of Miami that he hoped for an alumnus to donate the funds but "up to the present moment ...

nothing has arrived." Burton to Hughes, June 14, 1921, Burton Papers.

[17] Burton to Osborn, June 25, 1921; Osborn to Burton, June 25, 1921 tel., Chase Osborn Papers

[18] Burton to Osborn, July 1, 1921, Chase Osborn Papers.

[19] Beal to Osborn, July 19, 1921; White to Osborn, July 25, 1921; Osborn to Burton, Oct. 5, 1921; Burton to Osborn, Oct 11, 1921. In replying to Beal's thank you letter, Osborn further explained his motivation for making the gift: "I am not a rich man, but when the rich men failed to respond to President Burton's appeal, I felt I could not resist doing so. I really could not afford to make the subscription neither could I afford not to. You have no doubt found, as I have, that President Burton is quite irresistible." Osborn to Beal, July 22, 1921, Chase Osborn Papers.

[20] Burton to Frost, June 29 tel. and Burton to Frost, June 29, 1921, Burton Papers.

[21] *The Michigan Alumnus*, XXVII, Aug. 1921, pp. 599-601; *The Wolverine*, July 5, 1921.

[22] Burton to Hughes, tel. June 29, 1921; Burton to Hughes, Burton Papers; Hughes to Burton, July 1, 1921; Hughes to Frost, July 1, 1921, R.H. Hughes Papers, Miami University Archives.

[23] Frost to Burton, July 7, 1921, Burton Papers.

[24] Assistant to the President to Frost, July 9; Burton to Frost, July 29, 1921, Burton Papers. In forwarding the Frost letter to Osborn, Burton also told him that he had written every alumnus who attended the special May meeting in Ann Arbor "saying that your generous gift of $5000 has made it possible for us to secure Mr. Robert Frost for the coming year, and pointing to this gift and this plan as one definite result of our Alumni Conference." Burton to Osborn, July 29, 1921, Chase Osborn Papers.

[25] *The Wolverine*, Aug. 16, 1921.

[26] Bursley to Frost, July 9, 1921; Bursley to Burton, July 9, 1921. Burton told Bursley "how pleased I am with the way you have handled this matter." Burton to Bursley, July 18, 1921, Burton Papers. This scrap of paper is in folder 10, box 6 of the Burton Papers. The D'Ooge house is no longer extant.

[27] Frost to Untermeyer, Aug. 8; 20, 1921 cited in Louis Untermeyer, *The Letters of Robert Frost* (New York: Holt, Rinehart and Winston, 1963), pp.132, 134-5 hereinafter cited as Untermeyer, *Letters*.

[28] Frost to MacKaye, July 16, 1921 as cited in Lawrance Thompson,Ed. *Selected Letters of Robert Frost* (New York: Holt, Rinehart and Winston, 1964), pp.271-72 hereinafter cited as Thompson, *Selected Letters*. The Frosts nevertheless managed to get along without a servant.

[29] Burton to Frost, Oct. 6, 1921, Burton Papers; Thompson, *Frost 1915-1938*, p. 176.

[30] Stella [Brunt] to Mother, Oct. 15, 1921, Stella Brunt Osborn Papers, Bentley Historical Library, University of Michigan; *Michigan Daily*, Oct. 16, 1921.

[31] *Michigan Daily*, Nov. 15, 16, 1921.

[32] Stella [Brunt] to Mother, Nov. 19; Dec. 3, 1921; Jan. 27, 1922, Stella Brunt Osborn Papers.

[33] Frances Swain, "The Robert Frost of the *Whimsies* Evenings," *The Inlander*, V, no. 4 (April, 1925), pp. 24-28.

[34] *Whimsies*, Vol. II no. 1 Nov., 1921 p. 5; no. 3 April, 1922 pp. 3-4; Vol. III no. 1 Nov., 1922, p. 3.

[35] *Whimsies*, Vol. III no. 1 Nov., 1922, p.4; Thompson, *Robert Frost 1915-1938*, pp.178-183. Frost claimed that he was the real force behind this project: "I've got up this carnival for you, Carl, Amy, Vachel, and Bynner without anybody's knowing I was behind it. I had to be very indirect." Frost to Louis [Untermeyer], Feb. 23, 1922 cited in Untermeyer, *Letters*, p. 144.

[36] Thompson, *Robert Frost, 1915-1938*, pp. 179-180.

[37] *Ibid.* pp. 180-81.

[38] *Ibid.* pp. 181-182. Ibid. pp. 182-83. The lecture series is well summarized by Thompson and accompanying footnotes. Most of the material originated in the *Michigan Daily*, April 21; May 7, May 25, 1922.

⁴⁰Stella [Brunt] to Mother, Feb. 4, 1922, Stella Brunt Osborn Papers.

⁴¹Thompson, *Robert Frost 1915-1938*, p. 230; Stella [Brunt] to Mother, Oct. 22, 1921, Stella Brunt Osborn Papers; Lorch to Chase S. Osborn, Nov. 22, 1921, Chase Osborn Papers.

> Lorch's poem:
> Good Frost, we welcome you to this
> Our pretty little town,
> A place of science and of books,
> in art, of less renown.
>
> You bring to us fine comradeship,
> Your verse us all doth cheer,
> You come with Autumn colors,
> The poet's smile and tears
>
> Come, join the "Varsity" circle,
> It needs you through the year,
> We'll miss you when you leave us,
> Your memory we'll hold dear.

The Azazels actually did not invite Frost into membership until his third visit. Writing his friend Prof. Tilley: "It looks as if the Azazeels [sic] must have thought we got to be pretty good friends in my two years out there. I am grateful to them for still wanting me after having had me around so long on trial as it were. My warmest thanks to all of them." Frost to Tilley, no date but ca. 1925, Frost Collection, University of Michigan Library, Department of Special Collections hereinafter cited as Frost Collection.

⁴²Osborn to Burton, Oct. 25, 1921; Burton to Osborn, Oct. 17, Dec. 5, 1921, Chase Osborn Papers.

⁴³Thompson, *Robert Frost, 1915-1938*, p. 578 fn. 22; Osborn to M. L. Burton, Dec. 13, 1921, Chase Osborn Papers. Apparently Osborn did not meet Frost at this event for he asked Burton to pass along to Frost a bit of advice on improving his next presentation–something he would not have been shy to do himself if he had had the opportunity.

⁴⁴*Boston Herald*, June 22, 1922 (clipping in Burton Papers); Frost to Untermeyer, May 2, 1922 cited in Untermeyer, *Letters*, pp. 147-48; "Robert Frost's Opinion of a Merciful God. He Looks upon Pestilence, Disease and Wars as Interpositions of Divine Providence," *Washtenaw Post*, Oct. 27, 1921 as cited by Thompson, *Robert Frost, 1915-1938*, pp.177-78 and fn. 10, p. 577.

⁴⁵Burton to Roy W. Cowden, May 15, 1922; Lawrence H. Conrad [and 22 other signers] to Burton, April 27, 1922, Burton Papers.

⁴⁶*Presidents Reports, 1921-1922*, pp 90-91; Effinger and others to Burton, April 19, 1922; M.E. Cooley to A. E. White, July 7, 1922, Burton Papers; *Michigan Daily*, April 21, 1922; Thompson, *Robert Frost, 1915-1938*, p. 183.

⁴⁷Burton to Frost, Jan. 22, 1922, Burton Papers; Thompson, *Robert Frost, 1915-1938*, pp. 184, fn. 31, pp. 580-81. In 1962 the University awarded Frost the honorary degree of Doctor of Laws. See also endnote 79.

⁴⁸Thompson, Robert Frost, 1915-1938, pp. 184-86.

⁴⁹Frost to Untermeyer, May 2; July 8, 1922 in Untermeyer, *Letters*, pp. 147-49.

⁵⁰Frost to John T. Bartlett, [c.June, 1922] in Thompson, *Selected Letters*, pp. 279-80; Thompson, *Robert Frost, 1915-1938*, p. 188.

⁵¹Stella to Mother, Oct. 15, 1921; Osborn to Brunt, Oct. 4, 1921; Burton to Brunt, Oct. 11, 1921, Stella Brunt Osborn Papers; M.F. Hadrich [Osborn's secretary] to M.L. Burton, Oct. 5, 1921 enclosing Brunt to Osborn letter, Sept. 27, 1921, Burton Papers.

⁵²Osborn to Stella Brunt, Feb. 2, March 6, 12, 27, July 20, 30, Aug. 2, 1922; Stella to Mother, July 22,

1922, Stella Brunt Osborn Papers. The marriage and biographical data came from the files of the Bentley Historical Library. I knew Mrs. Stellanova Osborn well. She was an intelligent and interesting lady who was much committed to the Atlantic Union movement as a way to promote world peace. She was a generous contributor both of materials and funds to the Bentley Library and received an honorary degree from the University of Michigan in 1978. Her affection for Frost never wavered. When visiting Ann Arbor in April 1962, Frost gave her a copy of his volume of poetry for young readers, *You Come Too* (New York: Holt, Rinehart, Winston, 1961) inscribed: "To Stella Osborn from Robert Frost who was brought to Ann Arbor by Gov. Osborn in 1921 where so much happened." The volume is in the Bentley Library.

[53] University of Michigan, *Proceedings of the Board of Regents*, April Meeting 1922, p. 451, hereinafter cited as *Regents Proceedings*; Emil Lorch to Burton, March 20; Burton to Effinger, Hugh Cabot and A. H. Lloyd, April 6; Effinger, Cabot and Lloyd to Burton, April 13, 1922, Burton Papers.

[54] Thompson, *Robert Frost, 1915-1938*, pp. 200-201; Burton to Frost, May 4; Osborn to Burton, May 31; Burton to Osborn, June 24, 1922, Burton Papers.

[55] *Regents Proceedings*, October Meeting 1922, p.634; Burton to H. H. Rackham, June 23, 1923; Draft letter prepared by Burton June 21, 1923 addressed to Regents, Burton Papers.

[56] Thompson, *Robert Frost, 1915 1938*, pp. 202-209, 213-215; *Michigan Daily*, Oct. 10, 13, 1922.

[57] Frost to Sidney Cox [April 30, 1923] quoted in Thompson, *Robert Frost 1915-1938*, p. 591 and pp. 215-216, 224-225; Lawrence Conrad to Brunt, Stella Brunt Osborn Papers; Burton to Junius Beal and Walter Sawyer, July 28, 1923, Burton Papers.

[58] Junius E. Beal to M. L. Burton, June 29, 1923, Marion L Burton Papers. Beal added "[He] apparently did not take it seriously enough."

[59] Conrad to M. L. Burton, May 22, 1923 as cited in Thompson, *Robert Frost, 1915-1938*, pp. 225-29, 245, 591; *President's Report, 1923-1923*, p. 113.

[60] Burton to Dean J. R. Effinger, July 17, 1923; Burton to Regents Junius Beal and Walter Sawyer, July 28, 1923, Burton Papers. For Effinger's and faculty's views on Burton's candidates and possible problems of having a British holder of the fellowship see Effinger to Burton, July 20, 1923, College of Literature, Science and the Arts Records, Box 12, Bentley Historical Library.

[61] *President's Report, 1923-1924*, pp. 54-55; Burton to Bridges, June 25, 1924 and other correspondence in Box 13, folder 19, Burton Papers; *Michigan Daily*, April 2, 3, 5, 1924; Video, "Robert Frost at Hill Auditorium," [1962], Bentley Historical Library.

[62] Burton to Effinger, Lloyd, Cabot, Strauss, Robbins, July 15, 1924; Special Committee [members cited above] to Burton, July 17, 1924; Telegrams: Burton to Frost, July 27; Frost to Burton, July 29, July 30, Aug. 6, 1924; Burton to George P. Baker, Oct. 7, Baker to Burton, Oct.11, 1924, Burton Papers. Frost followed up his telegraphed recommendation of Williams with a long hand-written letter to Robbins (for passing along to Burton) strongly praising him. Frost to Frank Robbins, Aug. 25, 1924, Burton Papers.

[63] Burton to Frank E. Robbins, Aug. 25, 1924, Burton Papers; Further efforts to obtain a fellow for 1924-25 were limited and ceased altogether after Burton's death on February 18, 1925. Burton's death did not end the Fellowship in Creative Arts. Acting president Alfred Lloyd implemented Frost's suggestion of Jesse Lynch Williams offering him the position in June of 1925. Williams accepted and remained in Ann Arbor from the fall of 1925 until April of 1926. The new president, Clarence Cook Little wrote the Regents in 1928 that funds had lapsed for the Fellowship but proposed that it be resurrected in a different form. Little, in fact, was proposing something quite different–visiting professorships. He suggested the University try to obtain T.S. Eliot for a term and J.B.S. Haldane, an English biochemist for another. This was a far cry from Burton's idea. The Fellowship in the Creative Arts was gone. A.H. Lloyd to Williams, tel. June 30, 1925; Williams to Frank E. Robbins, Aug 3, 1925 copy in Box 3, folder 27; Little to Regents Gore, Stone, Clement, Murfin, Hanchett, Hubbard July 26, 1928, Clarence Cook Little Papers, Bentley Historical Library.

[64] Frost to Tilley, Feb. 20, and undated, 1924, Frost Collection.

[65] Burton to Effinger, July 16, 1924; Effinger to Burton, July 17, 1924, College of L.S.& A. Records, Bentley Historical Library.

[66] Frost to Burton, Sept. 24, 1924 attached to Burton to Effinger; Effinger to Burton, Sept. 30, 1924; College of L.S.& A. Records; Thompson, *Robert Frost, 1915-1938*, pp. 263-67.

[67] *Regents Proceedings*, September 1924 Meeting, p.416. Burton to Frost, Oct. 4, 1924 attached to Burton to Effinger, Oct. 4, 1924, L.S. & A. Records, Bentley Historical Library; *Michigan Daily*, Oct. 10, 12, 1924. The *Daily* editorialized that Frost's appointment was a "significant step in the progress of the University as a center of art and intellectual development."

[68] *Presidents Reports, 1925-1926*, pp. 36-40, 60; Thompson, *Robert Frost, 1915-1938*, p. 270, fn. 3, pp. 611-12.

[69] Frost to Louis N. Straus, Nov. 10, 1924, Frost Collection; Frost to Wenley, Dec. 12, 1924, Wenley Papers, Bentley Historical Library.

[70] Lloyd to Frost, April 10, 1925; Frost to Lloyd, April 20, 1925, Clarence Cook Little Papers, Bentley Historical Library.

[71] Burton Memorial Program, Vertical File of the Bentley Historical Library; *Detroit News*, May 29, 1925; Thompson, *Robert Frost, 1915-1938*, pp.279-280. Thompson writes further: "The poet had stretched the truth considerably when he assured these listeners, 'Remember now that I am telling you almost his very words.' In a sense his primary theme throughout his address had been the justification of the unorthodox stance he [Frost] had taken at Amherst and would take when he returned to Ann Arbor that fall.... If anyone saw through his machinations, and chose to view the address as an *Apologia Pro Vita Sua*, academically, Frost could at least say that he himself deeply believed in these notions, and that he had already talked them over with President Burton, who seemed to like them." p. 280.

[72] Frost to Tilley,n.d. but 1925 prior to Feb. 18.; March 17, 1925; *Michigan Daily*, Oct. 4, 1925; Thompson, *Robert Frost*, 1915-1938, pp.282-83. Thompson's biography covers Frost's 1925-26 year in Ann Arbor fully and accurately in Chapter 20. The following paragraphs briefly summarize these pages.

[73] Frost to Bartlett, [c. 1 January 1926] in Thompson, ed. *Selected Letters*, p. 323.

[74] Frost to Untermeyer, Feb. 11, 1915 in Thompson, *Selected Letters*, pp. 325-26; Frost to Effinger, Feb. 7, 1926; Effinger to Frost, March 1, 1926, L.S. & A. Records, Bentley Historical Library. Frost also kept some speaking engagements in the region during this time. Thompson's biography has Frost returning to Ann Arbor "late in January of 1925" but it was closer to the middle of February of 1926.

[75] See footnote 19, pp. 619-20 of Thompson, *Robert Frost, 1915-1938;* Dorothy Tyler, "On Remembering Robert Frost in Ann Arbor," n.d. but ca. 1957, Dorothy Tyler Papers, Univ. of Michigan Special Collections. For a recent discussion of Frost as a teacher see: Jay Parini, "'One Long, Wild Conversation': Robert Frost as Teacher," *The Chronicle of Higher Education*, March 26, 1990, pp. B6-B7.

[76] Frost to Bartlett, [May 26, 1926], in Thompson, *Selected Letters*, pp. 328-30.

[77] Updike, "Poet on the Fault Line," *The New Yorker*, March 15, 1999, p. 90; Frost to Mary Cooley, Mar. 5, 1927; Oct. 4, 1961, Frost Collection; *Regents Proceedings*, March 1927 Meeting, p. 169; March 1928 Meeting, p. 508; *Michigan Daily*, March 30, 1928.

[78] Hosting this luncheon was Eric Walter, Secretary of the University, filling in for President Harlan Hatcher who was out of the country. Frost reminded Walter that he had received only an honorary M.A. from Michigan and would like an honorary Doctor of Laws degree. This conversation led to an invitation to Frost for the Spring Commencement where he received this honor just a few months before his death in January 1963, *Ann Arbor Observer*, Vol. 12, No. 3 (Nov. 1987), p.48; Dorothy Tyler Papers, Box 2, University of Michigan Library, Department of Special Collections; Video, "Robert Frost at Hill Auditorium," [1962], Bentley Historical Library.

The Executive Committee of the Friends of the Bentley Historical Library

Invites You to Membership

The Bentley Historical Library was built in 1972 to house the Michigan Historical Collections, founded in 1935. Through a major gift from Mrs. Arvella Bentley in 1972 and several gifts from the members of the Friends of the library, the Collections found a permanent home in the building named in honor of the late Alvin M. Bentley, Congressman and University of Michigan Regent. The Bentley Historical Library is a modern research institution charged with the responsibility for preserving historical source materials primarily related to the history of the state of Michigan, its citizens, and organizations.

Your membership in the Friends of the Bentley Historical Library assists the work of the library in the conservation, preservation, and restoration of the important historical manuscripts given to the library over the past years. Your support is needed and welcomed to support conservation and other ongoing library activities.

....

Name_____

Address_____

_____ Zip_____

Membership ❏ Annual: $25.00   ❏ Sustaining: $100.00
            ❏ Gift   ❏ Memorial gift

Amount_____

Are you a University of Michigan Alumnus/a?

❏ Yes: year_____   ❏ No

Please return this form with check to:
Bentley Historical Library
University of Michigan
1150 Beal Ave.
Ann Arbor, MI 48109-2113